I CAN HELP
Weather Watch

Viv Smith

W

FRANKLIN WATTS

LONDON • SYDNEY

First Published in 1999 by
Franklin Watts
This edition 2001

Franklin Watts
96 Leonard Street
London EC2A 4XD

© Franklin Watts 1999

Franklin Watts Australia
56 O'Riordan Street
Alexandria, Sydney
NSW 2015

Editor: Helen Lanz
Art Director: Robert Walster
Designer: Sally Boothroyd
Environmental consultant: John Baines
Commissioned photography: Steve Shott
Illustrations: Kim Woolley

Printed in Hong Kong

ISBN: 0 7496 4296 3
Dewey Decimal Number: 551.6
A CIP catalogue record for this book is
available from the British Library.

Picture Credits
Cover: Steve Shott
Interior pictures: Barry Lanz 15 t; Franklin
Watts 5 bl, 7, 26/Ray Moller; SCOPE
19 br; Still Pictures 8/Martha Cooper,
12/B & C Alexander, 14/Richard West,
16/Mike Jackson;. All other interior images
by Steve Shott.

The publishers would like to thank St
Leonard's Primary School, Stafford, for their
help and enthusiasm, especially Viv Smith
and Class 2S who feature in this series.

Thank you also to Still Pictures for
photographs supplied for this book.

Contents

Whatever the weather

Look out of the window. What is the weather like outside? Is it raining, frosty, windy, sunny, cloudy, showery, foggy, or is it snowing?

> **WATCH OUT!**
> Never look directly at the sun, even with sunglasses on. This can seriously harm your eyes.

How often this term have you had to stay in at playtime because it was pouring with rain?

We look at the weather to help us decide what we should wear and whether we will be able to go outside or not.

The weather affects what we do and how we live.

Take it in turns in your class to note down what the weather is like each day.

HAVE A GO!

Make a chart like this to help you keep a record of what the weather is like each day for a week.

DAY	DATE	WEATHER
Monday	1st March	Cloudy and cold
Tuesday	2nd March	Cloudy, with some sunshine
Wednesday	3rd March	Raining

What sort of weather did you record?

You may notice that when it's windy, it might be a calm, gentle wind, a strong wind, or perhaps a gusty wind, blowing in strong bursts. When it rains, it may be a light shower or a heavy rainstorm.

Note down these details on your chart too.

Weather changes from day to day and year to year. If you keep your weather chart for a number of months, check to see if the weather behaves how you would expect for the time of year.

FASCINATING FACT!

Weather is caused when the atmosphere (the thick layer of air that surrounds the earth) is warmed. The sun heats the earth's surface and the heat from the surface of the earth warms the atmosphere.

7

Red sky at night

Weather is changeable, but there are usually patterns of weather that we can expect at different times of the year.

SPRING   wet and windy, with some warmer sunny days

SUMMER   warm sunshine, thunder, with some rain

AUTUMN   frosty mornings, cooler days and nights, some sunshine

WINTER   cold, sometimes snow and ice, often wet and foggy

Be a good weather watcher. Find out if the season's weather is different from the general descriptions above.

We may expect there to be rainy showers at certain times of the year, but there may be rainy showers when we don't expect them too.

In Britain, the sunshine and showers in spring help to keep our gardens and countryside green and allow our crops to grow. The summer sun ripens the crops. Autumn winds spread plant and flower seeds. The winter frosts break up the soil and kill insects and disease that harm the crops in the fields.

There are lots of old sayings about the weather and seasons. Have you heard any of these?

Red sky at night, shepherd's delight. Red sky in the morning, shepherd's warning.

March winds, April showers, bring forth May flowers.

If the crows are nesting high, then the summer will be dry.

How many more can you find? Do you think they are all true?

FASCINATING FACT!

In Australia, the seasons are at different times of the year. When it is our summer, it is their winter. That means at Christmas time, when it is our winter, they are enjoying summer days. Just think, Christmas dinner could be a barbecue!

SEASONS CALENDAR.

HAVE A GO!

Make a 'seasons calendar'.

Draw a picture of the sort of weather you would expect to get in each month of the year.

Weather and work

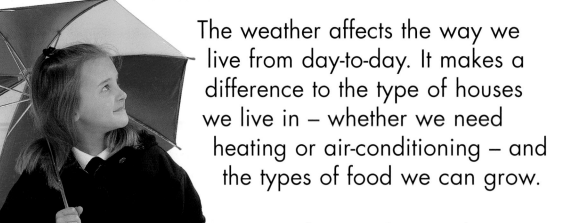

The weather affects the way we live from day-to-day. It makes a difference to the type of houses we live in – whether we need heating or air-conditioning – and the types of food we can grow.

The weather is also important for many people's work.

- Farmers need dry weather for harvesting, but enough rain for their crops to grow

- Strong winds can be dangerous for ships at sea.

- Lorry-drivers and motorway police need weather reports to tell them what it will be like to drive on the roads. Will it be foggy, icy, or will there be strong winds?

- Sports matches may be cancelled if it is snowy or too wet.

Can you think of anyone else whose job depends on the weather?

Why do you think a postman might be interested in what the weather will be like?

These people listen to the weather forecast. A forecast is when you say what is going to happen before it takes place. Getting a forecast right is not always easy.

Farmers and fishermen decide what they are going to do according to the weather forecast.

When the weather behaves differently to how we expect, it can cause many difficulties.

✂ HAVE A GO!

Study your local weather forecasts you see on television or hear on the radio. Make a diary of what the forecaster says and then record what the weather was actually like. Do this for a month. How often was the weather forecast right?

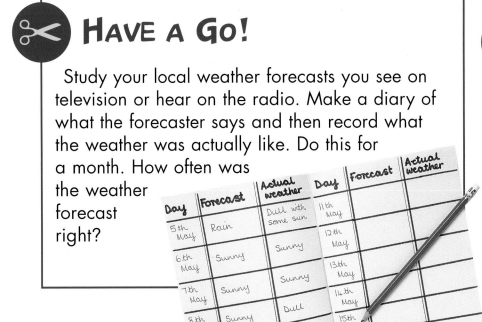

❗ FASCINATING FACT!

During January 1997, 92 aircraft, including Concorde, had to land in Manchester, rather than other airports in Britain and Europe, because of bad weather.

A change in the weather

Stand in a greenhouse or by a window on a sunny day. Feel how warm it gets. This is because the glass lets heat in much faster than the heat can get out. This is happening to the earth. The atmosphere, or the air around the earth, acts like a big greenhouse.

The Greenhouse Effect

When fuels are burned, carbon dioxide goes into the air. This adds to the carbon dioxide that is in the air naturally.

Carbon dioxide absorbs (takes in) the heat coming from the surface of the earth after it is heated by the sun.

This stops some of the heat from escaping into space.

The carbon dioxide acts like the glass in a greenhouse, so the heating up of the earth is called the greenhouse effect.

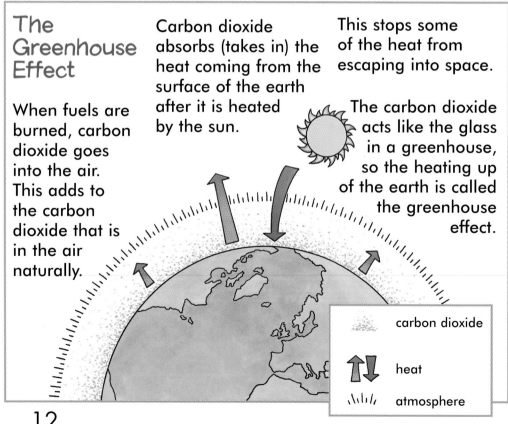

carbon dioxide

heat

atmosphere

Carbon dioxide is a gas that is in the air naturally. We add to it when we breathe it out (our bodies do not need it). It is also released into the air when we burn fuels such as coal, oil and gas.

Nature cannot absorb (take in) this extra carbon dioxide quickly enough. The more carbon dioxide there is, the more heat is kept around the earth. This changes the temperature of the earth – making it hotter. This is called global warming.

Global warming could also be making the weather change.

✂ HAVE A GO!

See the effects of global warming.

Make an 'island' out of modelling clay. Put it into a container. Pour in enough water to cover half of the island. Make a note of the water-level.

Add some ice-cubes. (These are like the ice and snow that lies on the land in the polar regions). Leave the container in a warm place. What happens to the ice-cubes? What happens to the level of the water?

! FASCINATING FACT!

Global warming could cause the ice on the land in the polar regions to melt. If this ice did melt, it would make the sea-levels rise. This could cause low-lying places to flood.

Keeping a balance

Some changes in the weather happen naturally.

When volcanoes erupt they throw out a lot of ash. If the eruption is big enough, this ash can be carried around the globe very high up in the sky. It can change weather patterns around the world.

Volcanic eruptions can cause heavy rainstorms. The rain can mix with the ash and make rivers of mud.

This statue in the Philippines is half covered in mud following a volcanic explosion.

Many gases are released during a volcanic eruption. Some of these gases mix with water vapour in the air and form a weak acid. This turns in to 'acid rain'.

In some countries, acid rain can damage wildlife and stone buildings.

Weather patterns changed before people were on the earth, and still change naturally. But it is thought that the pollution that we create has made changes in the weather speed up.

Weather records, such as the hottest, driest month or the wettest month, are being broken regularly.

In Britain, the weather in April 1998 was the wettest on record since 1818. It caused many floods.

✂ **HAVE A GO!**

No rain for a long time is called a drought. See what happens if plants do not get enough water. Grow two lots of cress in separate containers. When the cress has grown, water one container regularly but leave the other one alone. What happens?

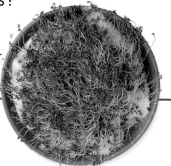

Too much of the same type of weather for too long can have terrible effects.

We cannot alter the way nature behaves, but we can alter the way we do things in order to help nature keep a balance.

15

Barbecues not bonfires

We can all help to cut down on pollution. This will help nature keep a balance.

The fumes from cars can cause a lot of pollution, especially smog. Smog is caused by sunlight changing the chemicals in car fumes. But today most cars have 'catalytic converters'.

Motorbikes and cars burn petrol to make them go. This adds to greenhouse gases.

A catalytic converter changes the fumes that come out of cars. It makes the harmful gases less dangerous.

You can help reduce car pollution by asking your parents to have your car checked regularly. This will help to make sure it is working properly.

 **LOOK BACK**

Cars use oil to make them work. Look back to page 12 to find out what happens when oil is burned.

Burning anything also makes the air dirty. It is not a good idea to have a bonfire, because this adds to the greenhouse gases. But it is OK to have a barbecue.

✂ HAVE A GO!

If your rubbish or garden waste is burned, it adds to the greenhouse gases. A lot of your garden waste could probably go on to a compost heap. This is plant and vegetable waste that rots down. It can be put on the soil to make other plants grow.

Usually, the fuel used for a barbecue has had a lot of the things that pollute the air taken out.

Use your own energy

Saving energy is another way to cut down on pollution.

To use energy, we burn fuels such as coal, oil and gas. When these fuels are burned, they release many gases, including carbon dioxide. So the less energy we use, the less fuel we need to burn and the less pollution we cause.

Here are some ways we can all help to save energy.

Walk, don't ride
Walking doesn't use up any energy – except your own – so it doesn't cause any pollution.

If you don't want to walk, why not cycle? Cycling doesn't cause pollution either.

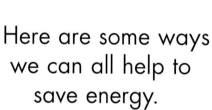

Take the bus

If your journey is too far to walk or cycle, why not take the bus? This means that lots of people are being moved about in just one vehicle, rather than only a few people in lots of cars. So less pollution.

Switch it off

If you're playing on your computer, or watching the television, turn it off when you've finished. Remember to turn off the lights too.

Use it again

Before you throw something away, check that you can't use it again. Perhaps it could be recycled and made into something else. This means that we cut down on the energy needed to make new things.

Take clothes to a charity shop. Someone else might want what you are throwing away.

19

Refreshing rain

If we cut down on pollution, our weather may slowly become cleaner and safer. It's much better to have clean, refreshing rain to fill our rivers and to water our crops.

But like the gases from volcanoes, gases in the fumes from factories and cars, lorries and aeroplanes, mix with the water droplets in clouds to form acid rain.

FASCINATING FACT!

The pollution we create in our own country doesn't just affect us. It is blown by the wind across the globe into other countries, where it forms acid rain.

Acid rain in Sweden and Norway comes mostly from pollution made in Britain and Germany. The acid rain in Canada comes from pollution blown over from the USA.

HAVE A GO!

On a globe or an atlas find the countries where acid rain is a problem.

If you have a weather computer program at school you could use this to help you study wind patterns.

✂ Have a Go!

You can make your own wind-vane so you can watch it blow in the wind to see where the wind is coming from.

You will need to ask an adult to help.

You will need:
* some card
* a plastic straw
* a pin and a bead with a hole in it
* a wooden pole
* safety scissors and a pencil

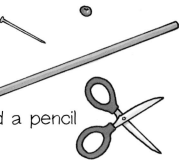

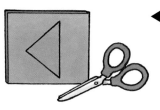 ◀ **1.** Draw a triangle onto the card. Cut it out carefully. This forms the front of your wind-vane.

2. Draw a shape like this onto the card. ▶ Cut it out carefully. This forms the back of your wind-vane.

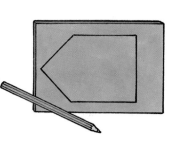

◀ **3.** Ask an adult to carefully cut a 1cm slit into both ends of the straw.

4. Push the arrow ▶ head in at one end and the end of the arrow at the other end. →

←

5. Stick the pin through the straw, through the bead and into the wooden pole. Do not push the pin in too tightly.

Now your wind-vane is ready to put outside to blow in the wind.

To check which way the wind is blowing, remember, a west wind blows from the west.

CFCs and the sun

In the atmosphere surrounding the earth there is a gas called ozone. This gas is very important because it helps to protects us from the harmful parts of the sun's rays.

But layers of ozone gas are being damaged by gases that are used every day. These gases are called CFCs.

FASCINATING FACT!

CFCs are in refrigerators and air-conditioning systems. They only cause a problem if they leak into the air.

We can help to stop this happening by being careful with old fridges, making sure they are thrown away properly. Contact your local council to find out how to get rid of your old fridge safely.

FASCINATING FACT!

CFC gases are in the cooling units of fridges. If they escape into the air, they can stay in the atmosphere for over 100 years.

22

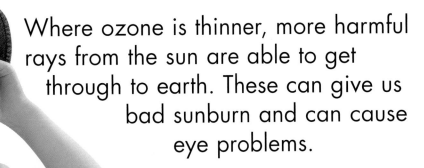

Where ozone is thinner, more harmful rays from the sun are able to get through to earth. These can give us bad sunburn and can cause eye problems.

We always need to be careful when we are out in the sun. But the sun's rays can cause us more harm if the ozone layer is damaged.

Be safe in the sun!

A few simple things

The weather happens whatever we do. But some of the things we do can affect the type of weather we get. And what the weather is like affects our lives.

We watch the weather so we can decide if we should put on our sun hats or wrap up warm.

We need to help nature to keep a balance.

Some problems seem so big that there may seem to be nothing we can do.

 HAVE A GO!

Make your own sun hat.
1. Cut out a rectangular strip of coloured paper. Fit this round your head to make the base of your hat. Mark where the ends meet. Tape the ends together.
2. Cut out a circle of paper to make the top of your hat. Stick this to the base.
3. Now cut out a peak and stick it on. Decorate!

But there are many simple things that we can do to help make a difference:

❀ Saving energy can help to reduce the amount of greenhouse gases in the air. Fewer greenhouse gases will help to slow global warming.

Turning off lights when they are not needed saves energy.

Do you leave your television on when you leave an empty room?

❀ Walking or cycling short journeys, instead of travelling in the car, helps to save energy and reduce pollution in the air. Less pollution means less acid rain. Be safe – walk or cycle with an adult.

❀ Be ozone-friendly – help the ozone to help us!

 LOOK BACK

Look back to pages 12, 13, 14, 15 and 20 and read about changes in the weather.

✂ **HAVE A GO!**

By watching our weather, we can check to see if it's changing or if it's doing what we would expect it to do.

Draw a large outline of the map of Britain. Make some weather symbols for sun, rain, snow and any others you can think of. Listen to the forecast each morning, then take it in turns in your class to be the day's weather presenter.

More activities and facts

 HAVE A GO!

Make static electricity by combing your hair quickly with a plastic comb, or pull a nylon sweater off over your head in a dark room. You will hear a crackle and may even see tiny flashes of electritiy, like small flashes of lightning.

FASCINATING FACT!

A rainbow is caused by sunlight shining through raindrops. The colours are always in the same order: with red on the outside, then orange, yellow, green, blue, indigo and violet.

 HAVE A GO!

Collect a large pine-cone and hang it outside somewhere. Watch to see what happens to it in dry weather, and what happens when the weather is wet.

FASCINATING FACT!

Lightning is made by static electricity that builds up inside a thundercloud as the water droplets crash into tiny bits of ice in the cloud. The lightning flashes in the cloud or between the cloud and the ground.

LOOK BACK

Look back to page 15 to find out what happens to plants when there is not enough water.

 ## HAVE A GO!

Lightning and thunder happen at the same time, but because light travels so much faster than sound, you see the flash first before you hear the thunder.

To find out how far away a thunderstorm is, count the seconds between seeing the lightning flash and hearing the thunder. Every 3 seconds represents 1km's distance.

✂ HAVE A GO!

Ask an adult to help you take a photograph of the same garden, piece of countryside, park or your nearest open-space in each of the four seasons. Compare the photographs. What differences do you see?

! FASCINATING FACT!

A desert is a very dry place. Not all deserts are hot. Parts of central Antarctica are cold deserts.

✂ HAVE A GO!

'Red sky at night, shepherd's delight.
Red sky in the morning, shepherd's warning.'

Find out how true this old saying is. Keep a record of the colour of the sky at sunset or sunrise. Then record what the following weather is like.

Useful words

acid rain: rainfall that absorbs (takes in) the pollution from burning fuels like oil and coal. Acid rain can damage wildlife and buildings.

atmosphere: the air surrounding the earth.

carbon dioxide: a gas that is in the air. Carbon dioxide adds to the greenhouse effect.

CFCs: cholorofluorocarbons. Gases used in refrigerators and air-conditioning systems. They can damage the ozone layer.

energy: power that gives us the ability to light things, heat and cool things, and to drive things such as machines.

foggy: when tiny drops of water in the air make it difficult to see.

frost: white, frozen drops of water that cover the ground when it is really cold.

fumes: smoke and gases which make the air dirty.

harvest: the gathering in of crops.

low-lying: something that lies close to the ground. Some countries lie only just above the level of the sea. If global warming melts ice at the poles and the sea level rises, these countries could become flooded.

polar region: the areas around the North and South poles.

pollution: something that makes land, water or air dirty.

recycle: to make something new out of something that has been used before.

release: to let something go or to give out something. When fuels are burned, they release, or give out, energy.

seasons: different times of the year. In Britain, the year is divided into four seasons; spring, summer, autumn and winter. Certain weather patterns are expected in each season.

Index